Highlights

W9-AWE-452

FIRST GRADE

1

AGES 6–7

Addition
Learning Fun Workbook

Copyright © 2020 by Highlights for Children. All rights reserved.
Reproduction of these pages is permitted for classroom use only. Otherwise, no part of
this book may be copied or reproduced without written permission of the publisher.

For information about permission to reproduce selections from this book for
an entire school or school district, please contact permissions@highlights.com.

Published by Highlights Learning • 815 Church Street • Honesdale, Pennsylvania 18431
ISBN: 978-1-68437-926-2
Mfg. 10/2019
Printed in Guangzhou, Guangdong, China
First edition
10 9 8 7 6 5 4 3 2 1

For assistance in the preparation of this book, the editors would like to thank:
Kristin Ward, MS Curriculum, Instruction, and Assessment; K–5 Mathematics and Science Instructional Coach
Jump Start Press, Inc.

Cookie Count

Everyone loves cookies! Count these cookies to solve the addition problems.

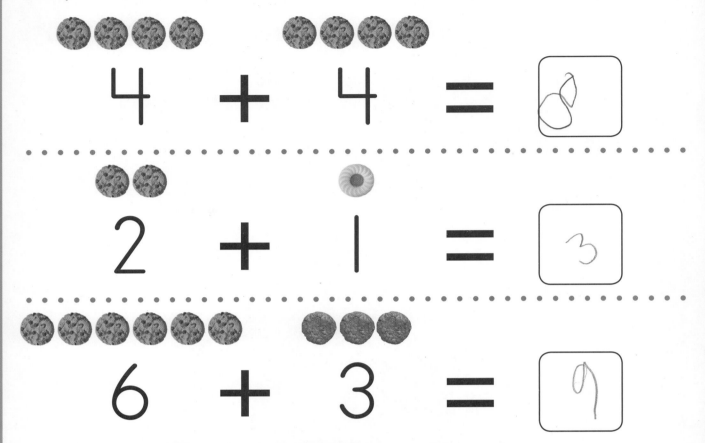

$4 + 4 = $ 8

$2 + 1 = $ 3

$6 + 3 = $ 9

Look for **22** cookies at this busy bakery. Cross off as you count.

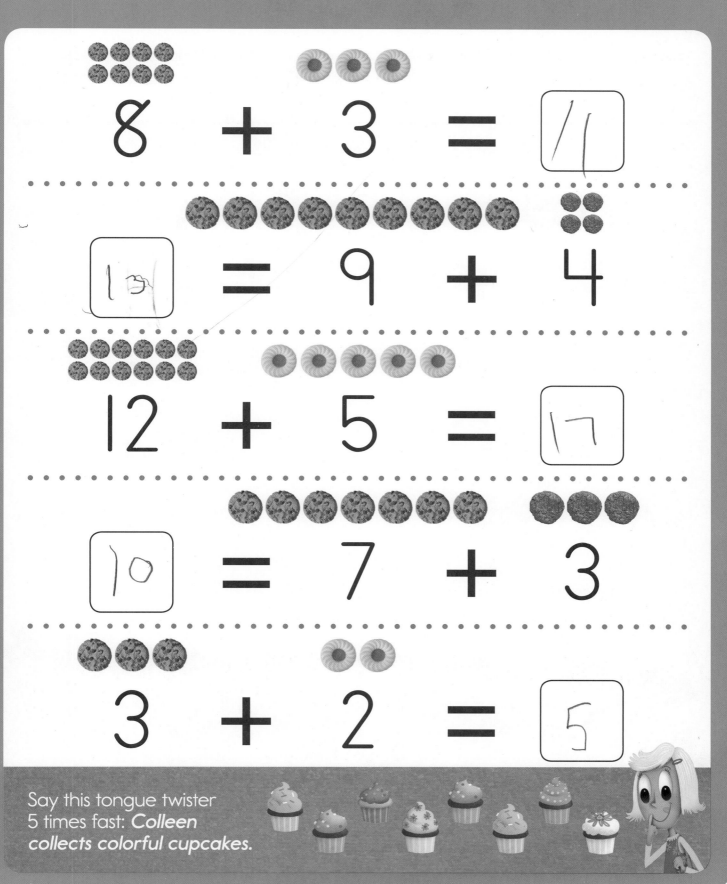

$8 + 3 = 11$

$13 = 9 + 4$

$12 + 5 = 17$

$10 = 7 + 3$

$3 + 2 = 5$

Hop to It!

You can use a number line to add. Start with the larger number. Then hop the number of spaces in the other number to find the sum. We did the first one.

$2 + 4 = \boxed{6}$ $2 + 10 = \boxed{}$

$3 + 2 = \boxed{}$ $\boxed{} = 5 + 8$

$3 + 4 = \boxed{}$ $9 + 5 = \boxed{}$

$\boxed{} = 6 + 3$ $5 + 12 = \boxed{}$

$7 + 9 = \boxed{}$ $\boxed{} = 14 + 6$

Find and circle each number that matches one of your answers.
Follow the sums to show Frannie the way to her log.

Kanga 2's

You can count on by 2's to find a sum.

Find the sum. Use the number line to help you. Then use the letters next to your answers to solve the riddle below. We did one to get you started.

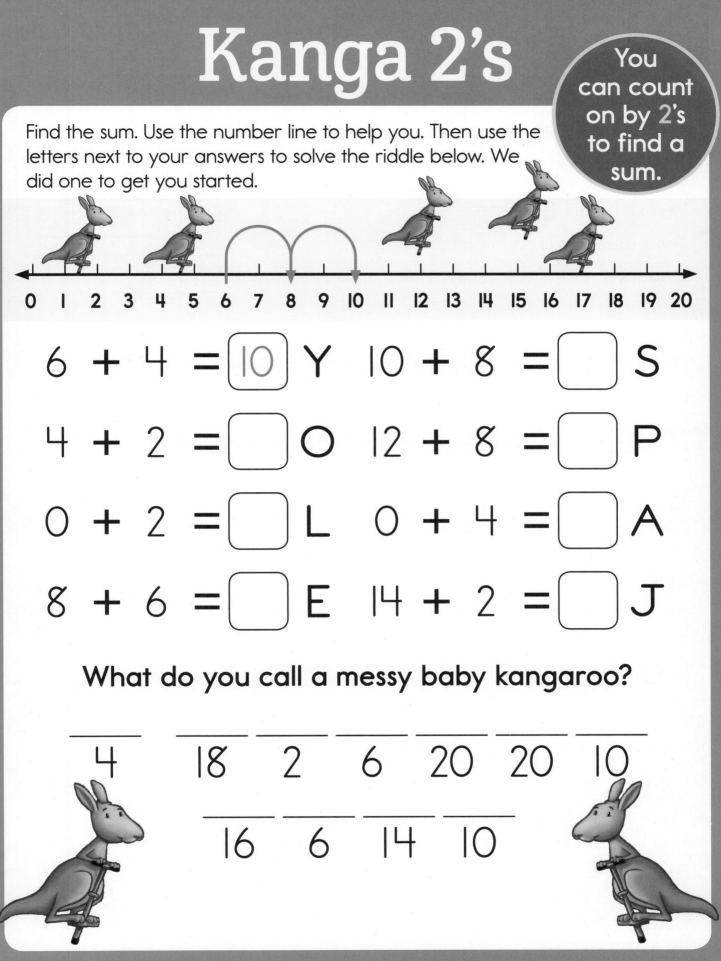

0 1 2 3 4 5 6 7 8 9 10 11 12 13 14 15 16 17 18 19 20

$6 + 4 = \boxed{10}$ Y $10 + 8 = \boxed{}$ S

$4 + 2 = \boxed{}$ O $12 + 8 = \boxed{}$ P

$0 + 2 = \boxed{}$ L $0 + 4 = \boxed{}$ A

$8 + 6 = \boxed{}$ E $14 + 2 = \boxed{}$ J

What do you call a messy baby kangaroo?

___ ___ ___ ___ ___ ___ ___
4   18   2   6   20   20   10

   ___ ___ ___ ___
   16   6   14   10

Frame It!

You can use 10-frames to show a problem. Here's how.

$10 + 1 = \boxed{?}$

First fill up the 10-frame.

Then add 1 circle to the next 10-frame.

Count on to find the sum.

$10 + 1 = \boxed{11}$

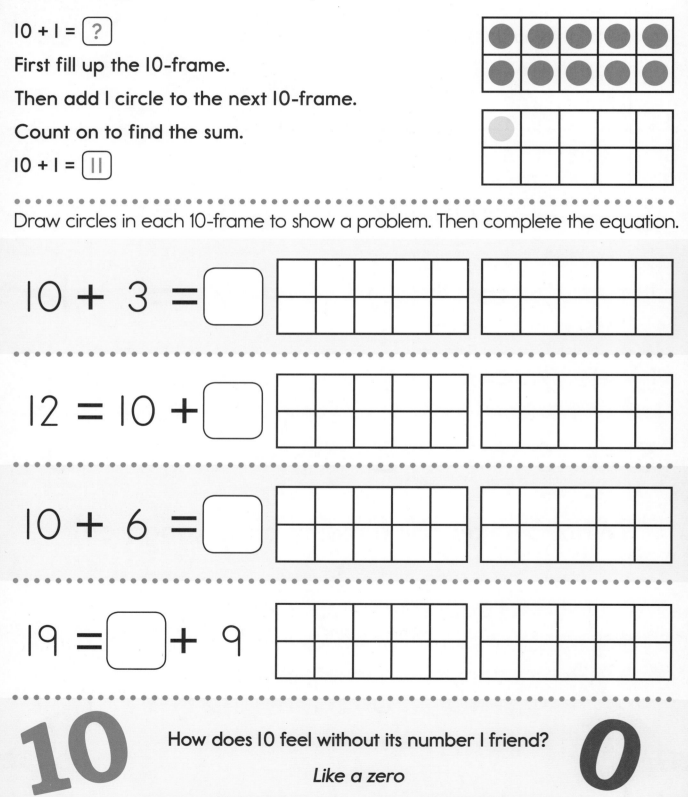

Draw circles in each 10-frame to show a problem. Then complete the equation.

$10 + 3 = \boxed{}$

$12 = 10 + \boxed{}$

$10 + 6 = \boxed{}$

$19 = \boxed{} + 9$

10   How does 10 feel without its number 1 friend?   **0**

Like a zero

You can make a 10 and then count on to add numbers within 20. Here's how.

$9 + 3 = \boxed{?}$

First show 9 in one frame. Then draw 3 yellow circles. Fill up the first frame, and draw any extras in the second frame.

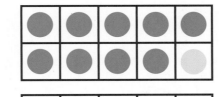

Now add the frames.

$10 + 2 = 12$, so $9 + 3 = \boxed{12}$

· ·

Your turn! The red circles are already drawn for you. Draw in the yellow circles to make a 10 and find the sum.

$\boxed{} = 8 + 4$

$6 + 5 = \boxed{}$

$7 + 6 = \boxed{}$

$\boxed{} = 9 + 8$

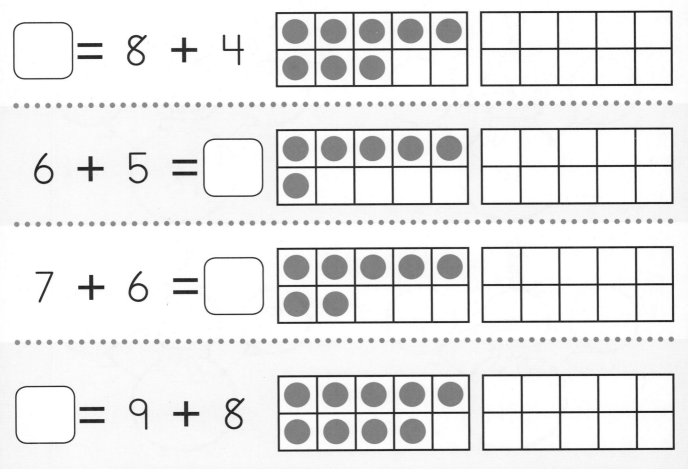

Make a Whole

A **number bond** shows how smaller numbers make up the larger number. You can use a number bond to find a missing part. Write in the missing parts in these number bonds. We did one to get you started.

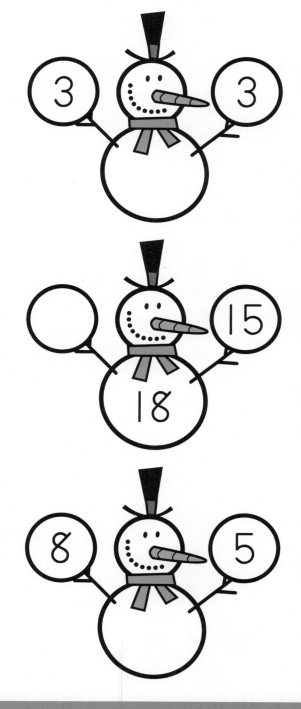

A **bar model** shows the parts (addends) that make up the whole (sum). Fill in each bar model to solve a put-together problem. We did one to get you started.

You can also use bar models to solve put-together problems.

6	3
9	

7	6

3	
10	

9	
18	

	2
8	

	1
12	

Which **3** pieces will finish the puzzle? Draw lines to place each piece.

9

Seeing Double

When you add doubles, you always get an even number.

The **2** numbers you add in a doubles fact are the same. Add these doubles. You can use a number line to help find each sum.

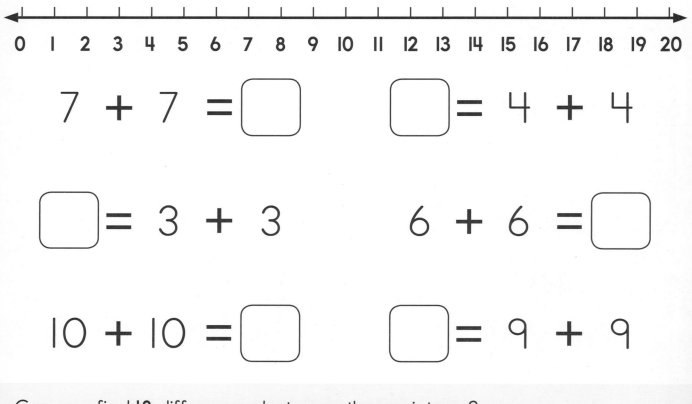

$$7 + 7 = \boxed{}$$

$$\boxed{} = 4 + 4$$

$$\boxed{} = 3 + 3$$

$$6 + 6 = \boxed{}$$

$$10 + 10 = \boxed{}$$

$$\boxed{} = 9 + 9$$

Can you find **18** differences between these pictures?

Doubles facts are easy to remember. That's why you can use them to do other addition problems that are near-doubles. For example, 6 + 6 is a double that equals 12. You know that 6 + 7 is 1 more, 13.

Use a doubles fact to help you add. Then use the letters next to your answers to solve the riddle below.

2 + 3 = ☐ W   3 + 4 = ☐ H

7 + 8 = ☐ U   6 + 5 = ☐ O

10 + 9 = ☐ D   5 + 4 = ☐ Y

What do you say when you meet a two-headed space alien?

"

__ __ __   __ __   __ __ __
7 11 5   19 11   9 11 15

__ __ ?   __ __ __   __ __
19 11   7   11 5   19 11

__ __ __   __ __ ?"
9 11 15   19 11

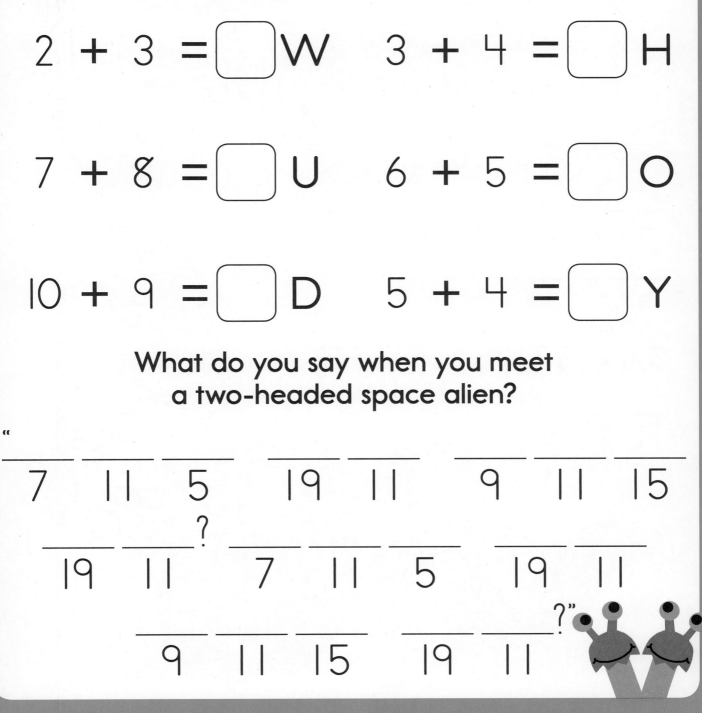

Reptile Riddle

Some addition and the code box will help you solve this riddle. Add the **2** numbers under each space, then fill that space with the letter from the code box that matches the answer.

What do two snakes do after they fight?

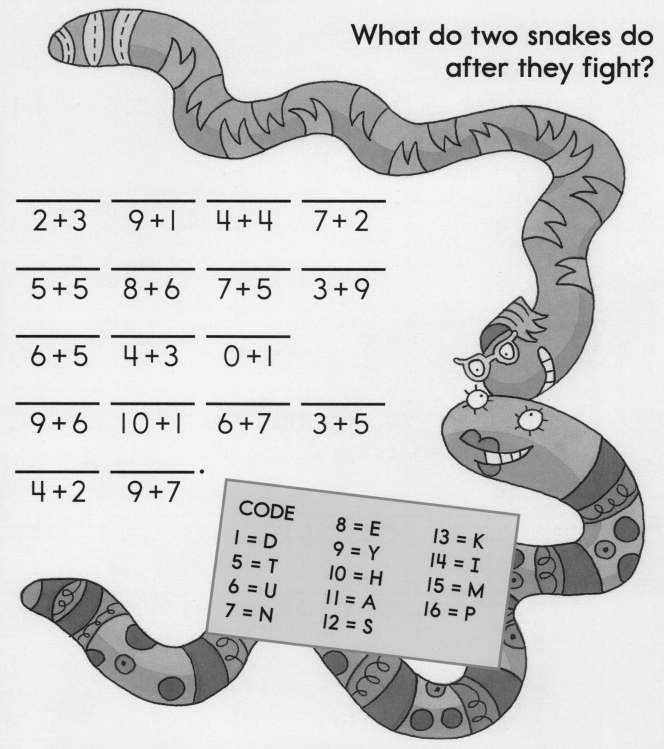

2 + 3	9 + 1	4 + 4	7 + 2
5 + 5	8 + 6	7 + 5	3 + 9
6 + 5	4 + 3	0 + 1	
9 + 6	10 + 1	6 + 7	3 + 5
4 + 2	9 + 7		

CODE

1 = D
5 = T
6 = U
7 = N

8 = E
9 = Y
10 = H
11 = A
12 = S

13 = K
14 = I
15 = M
16 = P

Key Problems

Solve these problems and use the code to answer the riddle. Then find **5** keys hidden on the island.

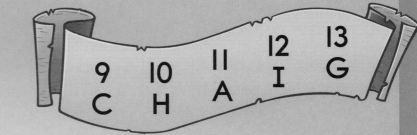

9	10	11	12	13
C	H	A	I	G

What did the pirate get on the test?

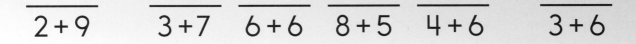

$$\overline{} \quad \overline{} \quad \overline{} \quad \overline{} \quad \overline{} \quad \overline{}$$

2+9   3+7   6+6   8+5   4+6   3+6

Happy Birthday!

Write an equation to solve each word problem.
Use the free space to show your thinking.

Tina and Tony are twins. They turned **6** years old today. They each have their own cake with the same number of candles. How many candles do they have in all?

To solve word problems, you can use different addition strategies, such as drawing circles to represent the items, using a number line, drawing in a 10-frame, or using number bonds or bar models.

Tina and Tony each received **3** gifts. How many gifts do they have in all?

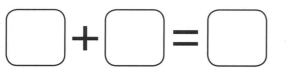

Find and circle the **10** objects in this Hidden Pictures puzzle.

baseball cap   spoon

crab   lizard

taxicab   funnel

hammer   paper bag

paddle   flag

Grandma cuts one cake into 10 slices. She cuts the other cake into 8 slices. How many slices of cake are there in all?

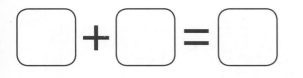 

At the party, **5** people each have a slice of chocolate cake, and **2** people have a slice of carrot cake. How many slices of cake were eaten in all?

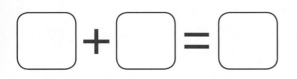 

Ice cream is served with the cake. **3** people have a scoop of strawberry and **1** person has a scoop of vanilla. How many scoops of ice cream were had in all?

Mom and Grandma each bought balloons for the party. Together, they bought **14** balloons. How many balloons could each have bought?

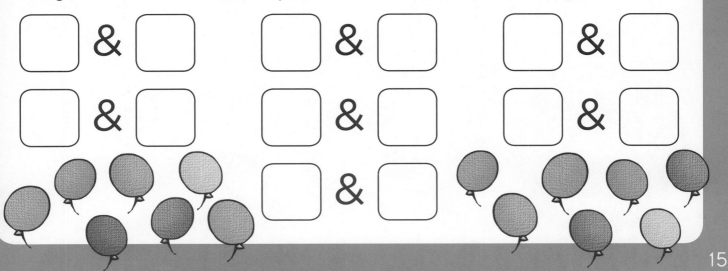

Flip Flops

When you add, you can change the order of the numbers, called **addends**, to make the problem easier! The sum is the same. Here's what that looks like if you draw a cube train.

$$1 + 3 = 4 \qquad 3 + 1 = 4$$

Find the sums. Then draw a line from each equation to the equation with flipped addends.

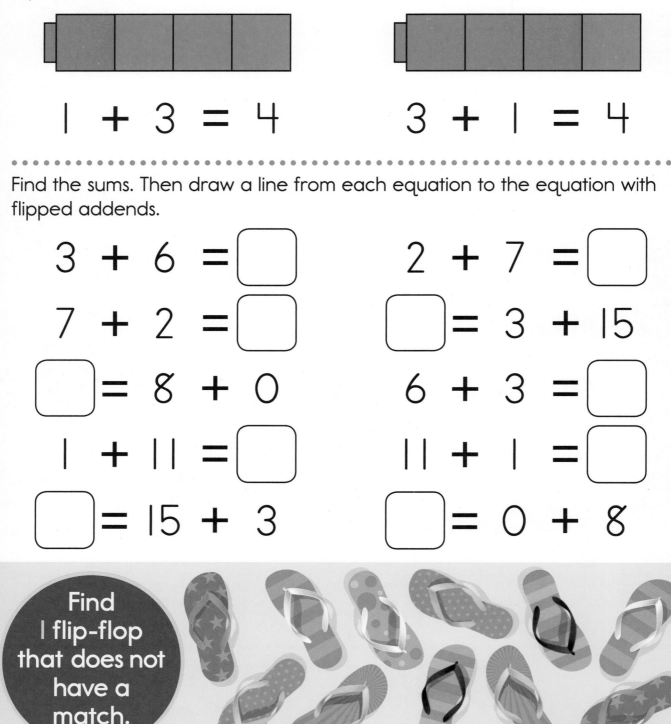

$3 + 6 = \boxed{}$ 　　 $2 + 7 = \boxed{}$

$7 + 2 = \boxed{}$ 　　 $\boxed{} = 3 + 15$

$\boxed{} = 8 + 0$ 　　 $6 + 3 = \boxed{}$

$1 + 11 = \boxed{}$ 　　 $11 + 1 = \boxed{}$

$\boxed{} = 15 + 3$ 　　 $\boxed{} = 0 + 8$

Find
1 flip-flop
that does not
have a
match.

Let's Balance!

An equation is **true**, or equal, if the sum is the same on both sides of the equal sign. An equation is **false**, or not equal, if a sum on one side of the equal sign is more or less than the sum on the other side.

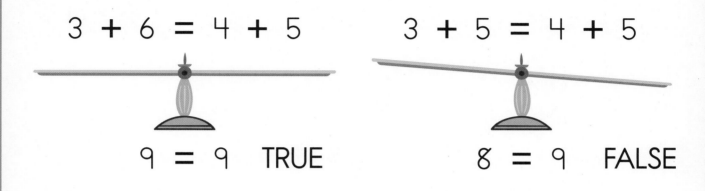

$$3 + 6 = 4 + 5$$

$$9 = 9 \quad \text{TRUE}$$

$$3 + 5 = 4 + 5$$

$$8 = 9 \quad \text{FALSE}$$

Help balance each scale! Fill in the missing numbers on the scales below to make each equation true. We did one to get you started.

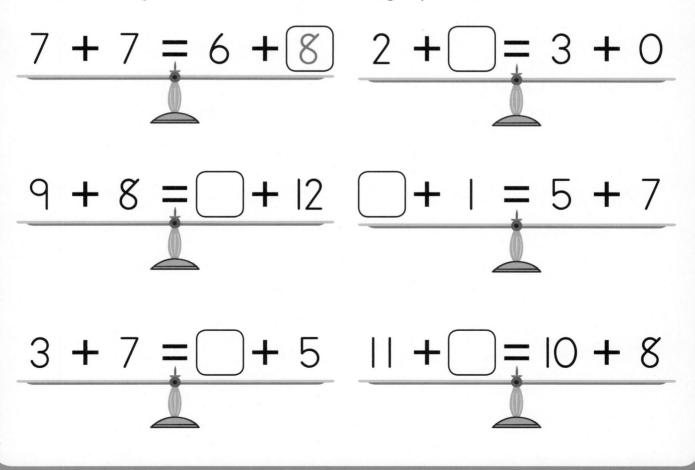

$$7 + 7 = 6 + \boxed{8}$$

$$2 + \boxed{} = 3 + 0$$

$$9 + 8 = \boxed{} + 12$$

$$\boxed{} + 1 = 5 + 7$$

$$3 + 7 = \boxed{} + 5$$

$$11 + \boxed{} = 10 + 8$$

Take Three

When you add 3 numbers, you can group 2 and add them in any order.

Find each sum. Use the space below each problem to show your thinking.

$$1 + 5 + 2 = \boxed{8}$$

$$\boxed{6} + \quad + \quad = \boxed{8}$$

$$\boxed{} = 5 + 1 + 3$$

$$1 + 3 + 2 = \boxed{}$$

$$4 + 6 + 2 = \boxed{}$$

$$3 + 2 + 6 = \boxed{}$$

$$\boxed{} = 1 + 3 + 4$$

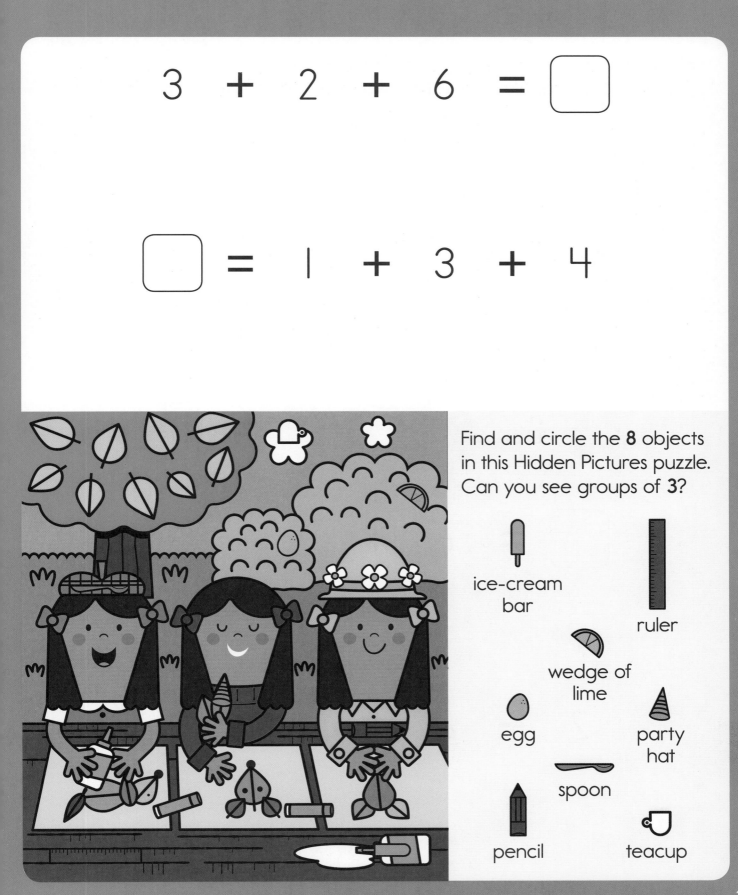

Find and circle the **8** objects in this Hidden Pictures puzzle. Can you see groups of **3**?

ice-cream bar

ruler

wedge of lime

egg

party hat

spoon

pencil

teacup

Fetch This!

Find each sum. Use the space below each problem to show your thinking. We did the first two to get you started.

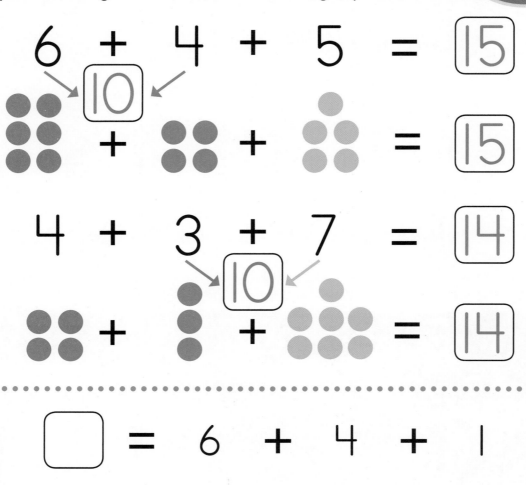

$6 + 4 + 5 = \boxed{15}$

$= \boxed{15}$

$4 + 3 + 7 = \boxed{14}$

$= \boxed{14}$

$\boxed{} = 6 + 4 + 1$

$2 + 8 + 4 = \boxed{}$

$$7 + 3 + 10 = \boxed{}$$

$$\boxed{} = 5 + 8 + 2$$

Find and circle 10 dogs in the park.

Toy Makers

You can add in any order to solve word problems with 3 numbers.

The toy makers had to fill a lot of orders last week! Write an equation to solve each word problem. Show your thinking. You can use any of the strategies you know.

On Monday, there were **8 red robots** , **3 blue robots** , and **I green robot** working at the toy factory. How many robots were working?

$$\boxed{} + \boxed{} + \boxed{} = \boxed{}$$

On Tuesday, **2 red robots** , **4 blue robots** , and **2 green robots** 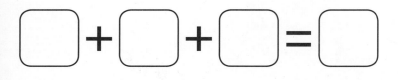 went to work. How many robots went to work?

$$\boxed{} + \boxed{} + \boxed{} = \boxed{}$$

On Wednesday, the workers made **I xylophone** , **5 teddy bears** , and **4 music boxes** . How many toys did the workers make?

$$\boxed{} + \boxed{} + \boxed{} = \boxed{}$$

On Thursday, Betty made **7 teddy bears** . On Friday, she made **7 teddy bears** . On Saturday, she made **6 teddy bears** . How many teddy bears did Betty make in all?

☐ + ☐ + ☐ = ☐

Robby packed a box with **4 red balls** , **11 blue balls** , and **5 green balls** . How many balls did Robby pack in the box?

☐ + ☐ + ☐ = ☐

What silly things do you see at the toy factory?

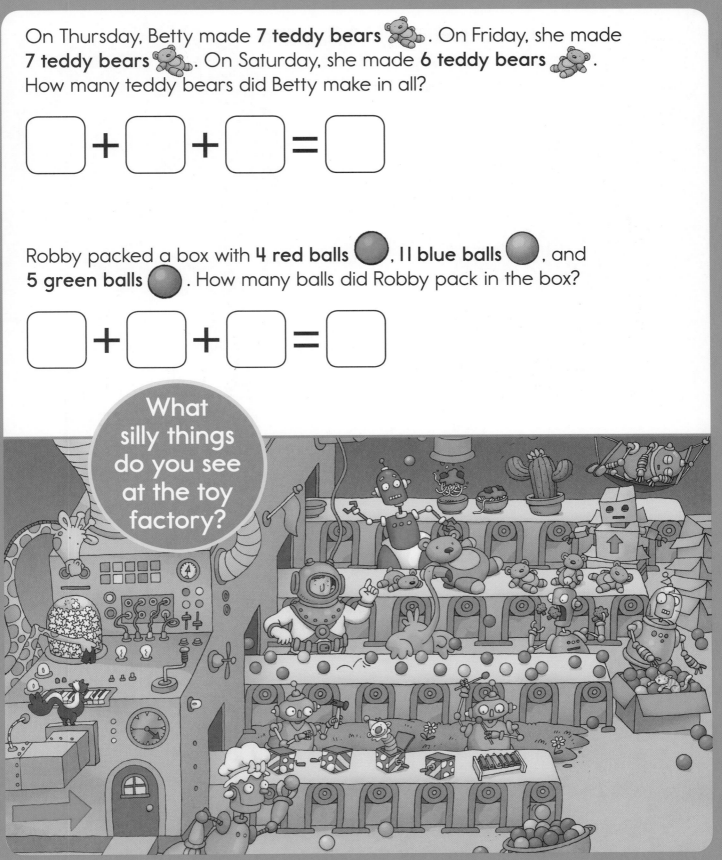

All in the Family

Welcome home! Use **fact families** to find missing numbers. Write the numbers to complete each family. We did the first one to get you started.

A fact family is a group of math facts using the same numbers. You can use fact families to help you solve equations.

House 1 (3, 5, 2)

$3 + 2 = \boxed{5}$

$\boxed{2} + 3 = 5$

$5 - \boxed{3} = 2$

$\boxed{5} - 2 = 3$

House 2 (1, 9, 8)

$8 + 1 = \boxed{}$

$\boxed{} + 8 = 9$

$9 - \boxed{} = 8$

$\boxed{} - 8 = 1$

House 3 (7, 11, 4)

$7 + \boxed{} = 11$

$4 + 7 = \boxed{}$

$\boxed{} - 7 = 4$

$11 - 4 = \boxed{}$

House 4 (6, 15, 9)

$6 + 9 = \boxed{}$

$\boxed{} + 6 = 15$

$\boxed{} - 6 = 9$

$15 - \boxed{} = 6$

Who can jump higher than a house?

Everyone! Houses can't jump.

Operations and Algebraic Thinking: Addition/Subtraction Relationship

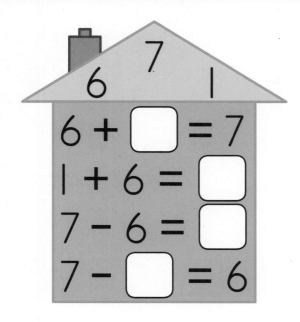

7
6   1

6 + □ = 7
1 + 6 = □
7 - 6 = □
7 - □ = 6

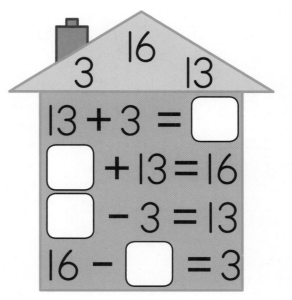

16
3   13

13 + 3 = □
□ + 13 = 16
□ - 3 = 13
16 - □ = 3

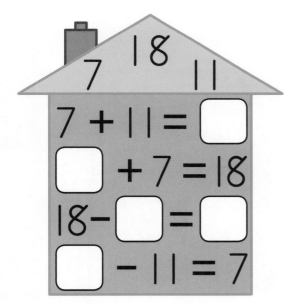

18
7   11

7 + 11 = □
□ + 7 = 18
18 - □ = □
□ - 11 = 7

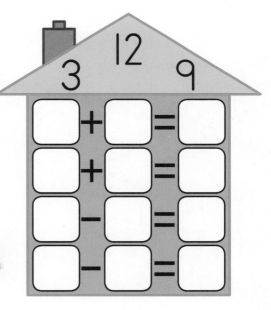

12
3   9

□ + □ = □
□ + □ = □
□ - □ = □
□ - □ = □

What did the family listen to on their road trip?
Car-tunes

25

Missing!

When an addend is missing, you can use subtraction to find it.

Be a fact-family detective! Find the addends missing in the addition problems. Show the subtraction in the fact family that can help you find the missing addend. We did the first one to get you started.

$$5 + \boxed{1} = 6$$
$$\boxed{6} - \boxed{5} = \boxed{1}$$

$$\boxed{} + 3 = 11$$
$$\boxed{} - \boxed{} = \boxed{}$$

$$\boxed{} + 2 = 9$$
$$\boxed{} - \boxed{} = \boxed{}$$

$$7 + \boxed{} = 16$$
$$\boxed{} - \boxed{} = \boxed{}$$

Help the monkey detectives find **20** missing bananas. The bananas are many different colors.

Operations and Algebraic Thinking: Addition/Subtraction Relationship

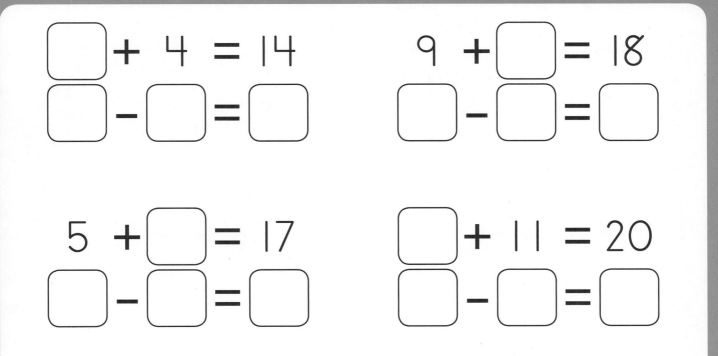

☐ + 4 = 14

9 + ☐ = 18

☐ − ☐ = ☐

☐ − ☐ = ☐

5 + ☐ = 17

☐ + 11 = 20

☐ − ☐ = ☐

☐ − ☐ = ☐

Compare these pictures. Circle what's missing at the second soccer game.

At the Cat Café

It's time for a cupcake break at Ms. Kitty's Cupcake Cafe! Draw to show how to solve each add-to word problem. Then write the equation.

There are **9 gray cats** 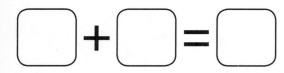 in the cafe. Then **3 orange cats** walk in. How many cats are now in the café?

☐ + ☐ = ☐

One way to think about addition is to "add to" a part to make a whole. You can use add-to to find a missing number.

Ms. Kitty sold **17 cupcakes** 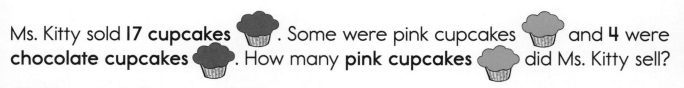 . Some were pink cupcakes and **4** were **chocolate cupcakes** . How many **pink cupcakes** did Ms. Kitty sell?

☐ + ☐ = ☐

Tabby bought some **cupcakes**  . He ate **2 cupcakes** . He has **8 left**. How many **cupcakes** did he have to start?

☐ + ☐ = ☐

What has eyes like a cat, a tail like a cat, and paws like a cat, but isn't a cat?

A kitten

Find and circle the **10** objects in this Hidden Pictures puzzle.
What do these objects have in common?

camera

candy
cane

crown

corn

cabbage

canoe

clothespin

crab

cactus

cloud

Guess What?

Mr. Count's math students are putting together some guessing jars. Each student brings different items to add to the jars. Draw to show how to find each missing number. You might use a number bond or bar model. Then complete the equation to solve the word problem.

Matt has **6 toy cars** . Ali has **3** more **toy cars** than Matt. How many toy cars does Ali have?

$$6 + 3 = \boxed{}$$

Hakim has **6** fewer **marbles** than Izzy has. Hakim has **8 marbles** . How many marbles does Izzy have?

$$6 + 8 = \boxed{}$$

Jen has **10 pieces of pasta** . Martin has **4 pieces of pasta** . How many more pieces of pasta does Jen have?

$$\boxed{} + 4 = 10$$

Kami has **10** fewer **mints**  than Brian has. Brian has **15 mints** . How many mints does Kami have?

$$10 + \boxed{} = 15$$

Rosa has **19** pieces of **candy corn** . Rico has **12** pieces of **candy corn** . How many more pieces of candy corn does Rosa have?

$$12 + \boxed{} = 19$$

The numbers below match the number of items in the jars. Use the clues to figure out how many items are in each jar.

- The toy cars are the smallest number.
- The candy-corn pieces are the biggest number.
- There are fewer mints than marbles.
- There are more pieces of bow-tie pasta than marbles.

toy cars

_____

mints

_____

candy-corn

_____

bow-tie pasta

_____

marbles

_____

136   53   100
320   9

High-Flying Tens

You can use a hundred chart to add tens.

$20 + 30 = \boxed{?}$

1	2	3	4	5	6	7	8	9	10
11	12	13	14	15	16	17	18	19	20
21	22	23	24	25	26	27	28	29	30
31	32	33	34	35	36	37	38	39	40
41	42	43	44	45	46	47	48	49	50
51	52	53	54	55	56	57	58	59	60
61	62	63	64	65	66	67	68	69	70
71	72	73	74	75	76	77	78	79	80
81	82	83	84	85	86	87	88	89	90
91	92	93	94	95	96	97	98	99	100

To add tens, start on 20.

Count on 3 tens.

So . . .
$20 + 30 = \boxed{50}$

Use the hundred chart to solve these equations.

$10 + 10 = \boxed{}$ $10 + 80 = \boxed{}$

$20 + 40 = \boxed{}$ $70 + 10 = \boxed{}$

$60 + 30 = \boxed{}$ $30 + 30 = \boxed{}$

$50 + 20 = \boxed{}$ $80 + 10 = \boxed{}$

50 + 10 = ☐   20 + 30 = ☐

41 + 30 = ☐   35 + 10 = ☐

92 + 10 = ☐   46 + 10 = ☐

Can you find **10** kites? Color in a kite as you find each one.

Summy Beach Day

You can use a hundred chart to add tens. You can also use a hundred chart to add a one-digit number to a two-digit number. Here's how.

$42 + 5 = \boxed{?}$

1	2	3	4	5	6	7	8	9	10
11	12	13	14	15	16	17	18	19	20
21	22	23	24	25	26	27	28	29	30
31	32	33	34	35	36	37	38	39	40
41	42	43	44	45	46	47	48	49	50
51	52	53	54	55	56	57	58	59	60
61	62	63	64	65	66	67	68	69	70
71	72	73	74	75	76	77	78	79	80
81	82	83	84	85	86	87	88	89	90
91	92	93	94	95	96	97	98	99	100

Start at 42.

Move right and count 5 boxes.

So . . .
$42 + 5 = \boxed{47}$

Solve each problem on this page and page 33. Then use the letters next to the answers to solve the riddle on the next page. We did the first one to get you started.

$79 + 4 = \boxed{83}$ A $39 + 8 = \boxed{}$ I

$65 + 9 = \boxed{}$ E $48 + 7 = \boxed{}$ L

$59 + 9 = \boxed{}$ F $61 + 30 = \boxed{}$ M

56 + 7 = ☐ G   27 + 3 = ☐ U

18 + 9 = ☐ O   77 + 7 = ☐ A

44 + 8 = ☐ P   43 + 6 = ☐ S

32 + 4 = ☐ R   91 + 2 = ☐ A

What should a math student always bring to the beach?

$$\overline{93}\quad \overline{52}\quad \overline{83}\quad \overline{47}\quad \overline{36}$$

$$\overline{27}\quad \overline{68}\quad \overline{49}\quad \overline{30}\quad \overline{91}\ -$$

$$\overline{63}\quad \overline{55}\quad \overline{84}\quad \overline{49}\quad \overline{49}\quad \overline{74}\quad \overline{49}$$

Get Building

You can draw or build **towers of ten** to add a two-digit number and a one-digit number. You can draw them stacking up or stacking across. Here's how.

$$22 + 4 = \boxed{26} \qquad \boxed{34} + 5 = \boxed{39}$$

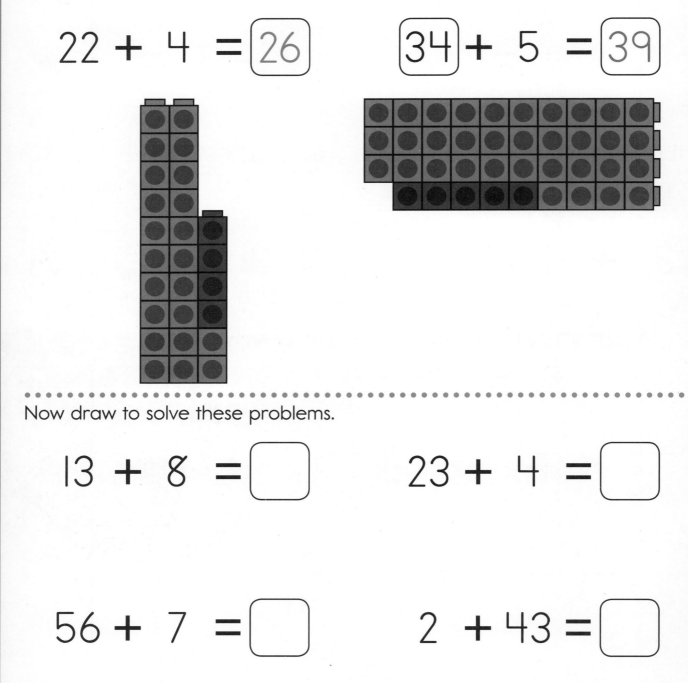

Now draw to solve these problems.

$$13 + 8 = \boxed{} \qquad 23 + 4 = \boxed{}$$

$$56 + 7 = \boxed{} \qquad 2 + 43 = \boxed{}$$

$9 + 82 =$ ☐ $6 + 94 =$ ☐

$9 + 31 =$ ☐ $28 + 4 =$ ☐

$76 + 7 =$ ☐ $63 + 3 =$ ☐

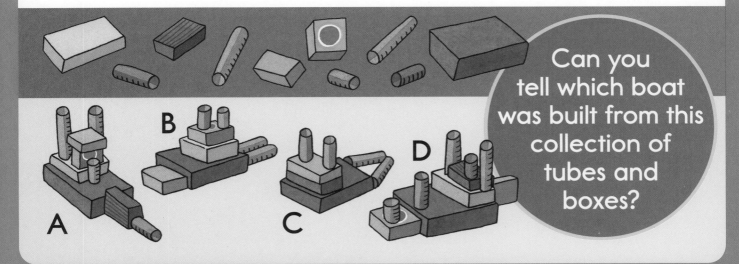

Can you tell which boat was built from this collection of tubes and boxes?

A   B   C   D

Hidden 10's

You can find hidden 10's to help you add!

Find each sum. Use the space below each problem to show your thinking.

$$51 + 9 = \boxed{}$$

Make a 10.

$$50 + 10 = \boxed{60}$$

So . . .

$$51 + 9 = \boxed{60}$$

· ·

$$28 + 2 = \boxed{}$$

$$16 + 4 = \boxed{}$$

$$33 + 7 = \boxed{}$$

$$42 + 8 = \boxed{}$$

Sometimes you need to break a number apart to make a 10.

$$64 + 8 = \boxed{}$$

$$64 + 6 + 2$$

$$60 + 10 + 2 = \boxed{72}$$

So... $64 + 8 = \boxed{72}$

$$38 + 4 = \boxed{}$$

Can you find **10** tennis balls in this picture?

$$55 + 7 = \boxed{}$$

Jump In!

You can jump along a number line to make a ten and add. Here's how.

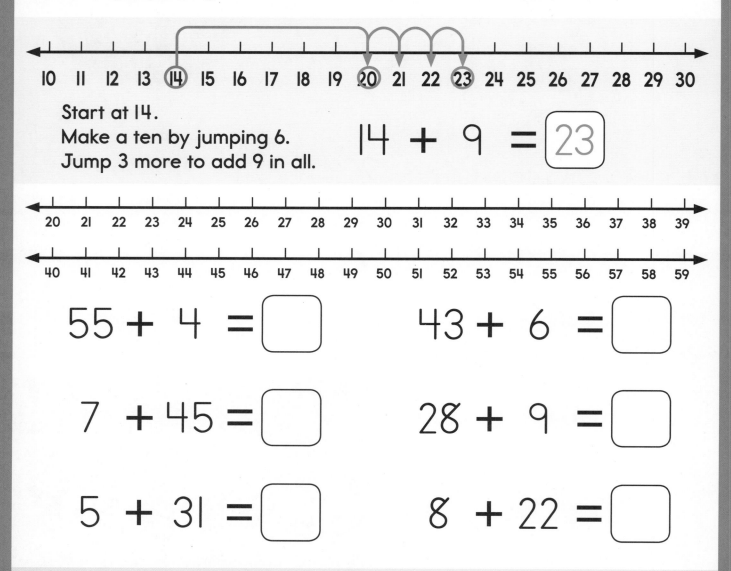

Start at 14.
Make a ten by jumping 6.
Jump 3 more to add 9 in all.

$14 + 9 = \boxed{23}$

$55 + 4 = \boxed{}$

$43 + 6 = \boxed{}$

$7 + 45 = \boxed{}$

$28 + 9 = \boxed{}$

$5 + 31 = \boxed{}$

$8 + 22 = \boxed{}$

These kids have jumbled their jump ropes. Trace the ropes to find out which kids are jump-rope partners. Then add each partner's numbers.

Number and Operations in Base Ten: Add Two-Digit and One-Digit Numbers

Get a Head Start

You can use mental math to count on or back by tens.

Use your head to find **10 less** and **10 more**.
We did the first one to get you started.

10 LESS		10 MORE
38	48	58
	83	
	19	
	76	

10 LESS		10 MORE
	21	
	55	
	64	
	90	

Color each space that has a number you wrote in the chart. Color the 10-less spaces blue. Color the 10-more spaces red. You'll see something that also uses your head!

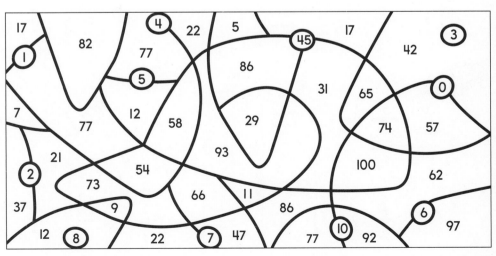

Math Path

Use the hundred chart to add. Count on by tens. Color the box on the chart for each answer you find. What you see might make you smile!

1	2	3	4	5	6	7	8	9	10
11	12	13	14	15	16	17	18	19	20
21	22	23	24	25	26	27	28	29	30
31	32	33	34	35	36	37	38	39	40
41	42	43	44	45	46	47	48	49	50
51	52	53	54	55	56	57	58	59	60
61	62	63	64	65	66	67	68	69	70
71	72	73	74	75	76	77	78	79	80
81	82	83	84	85	86	87	88	89	90
91	92	93	94	95	96	97	98	99	100

$4 + 10 = \boxed{}$ $29 + 20 = \boxed{}$

$2 + 40 = \boxed{}$ $22 + 30 = \boxed{}$

$6 + 80 = \boxed{}$ $4 + 20 = \boxed{}$

Number and Operations in Base Ten: Add Within 100

$19 + 40 = \boxed{}$ $37 + 40 = \boxed{}$

$15 + 70 = \boxed{}$ $33 + 30 = \boxed{}$

$24 + 50 = \boxed{}$ $58 + 10 = \boxed{}$

$7 + 10 = \boxed{}$ $7 + 20 = \boxed{}$

Help Matt find a path to his door. He can move to a new floor tile by **adding 5** or **subtracting 3**. He can move, up, down, left, or right, but not diagonally.

Get Growing!

Use a few of the addition strategies you've learned.

Nadia and Nate help out on their family's farm. Now it's time to gather some numbers. Solve these word problems about what's growing.

Nate planted **41 carrot seeds** 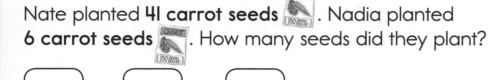. Nadia planted **6 carrot seeds** . How many seeds did they plant?

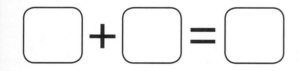

Nadia picked **19 green apples** . Nate picked **2 red apples** . How many apples did they pick in all?

○ + ○ = ○

What silly things do you see?

Mom gathered **32 carrots** 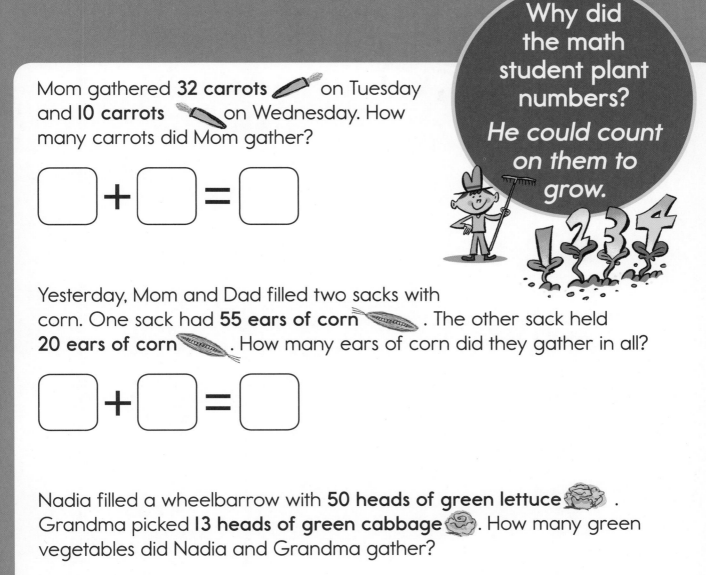 on Tuesday and **10 carrots** on Wednesday. How many carrots did Mom gather?

☐ + ☐ = ☐

Why did the math student plant numbers?

He could count on them to grow.

Yesterday, Mom and Dad filled two sacks with corn. One sack had **55 ears of corn** . The other sack held **20 ears of corn** . How many ears of corn did they gather in all?

☐ + ☐ = ☐

Nadia filled a wheelbarrow with **50 heads of green lettuce**  . Grandma picked **13 heads of green cabbage** . How many green vegetables did Nadia and Grandma gather?

☐ + ☐ = ☐

Later, Nate and Nadia had to weed the garden. They each pulled out **7 weeds**  . How many weeds did they pull out all together?

☐ + ☐ = ☐

Congratulations!

Highlights

FIRST GRADE 1

_____
(your name)

worked hard
and finished the

Addition
Learning Fun Workbook

Answers

Inside Front Cover

5	10	15	35	50	40
15	90	20	25	60	20
70	75	20	30	15	40
20	45	40	35	80	20
25	50	15	20	90	50
35	55	60	65	70	75

Pages 2–3
Cookie Count

4+4=8
2+1=3
6+3=9
8+3=11
13=9+4
12+5=17
10=7+3
3+2=5

Page 4
Hop to It!

2+2=6
3+2=5
3+4=7
9=6+3
7+9=16
2+10=12
13=5+8
9+5=14
5+12=17
20=14+6

START
FINISH

Page 5
Kanga 2's

6+4=10 **Y**
4+2=6 **O**
0+2=2 **L**
8+6=14 **E**
10+8=18 **S**
12+8=20 **P**
0+4=4 **A**
14+2=16 **J**

What do you call a messy baby kangaroo?
A SLOPPY JOEY

Pages 6–7
Frame It!

10+3=13
12=10+2
10+6=16
19=10+9
12=8+4
6+5=11
7+6=13
17=9+8

6	3
9	

7	6
13	

3	7
10	

9	9
18	

6	2
8	

11	1
12	

Pages 8–9
Make a Whole

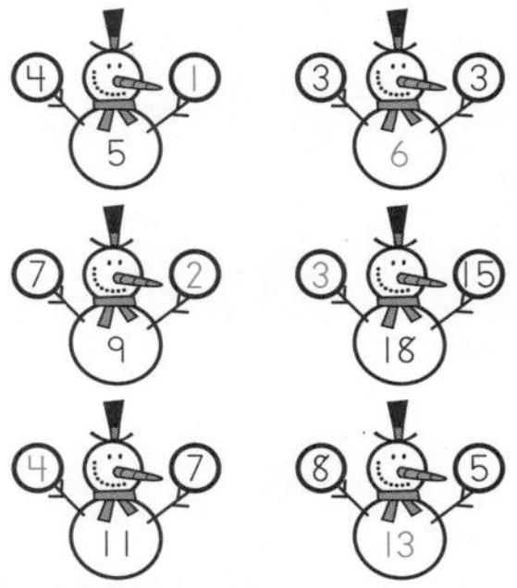
4
1
5
3
3
6
7
2
9
3
15
18
4
7
11
8
5
13

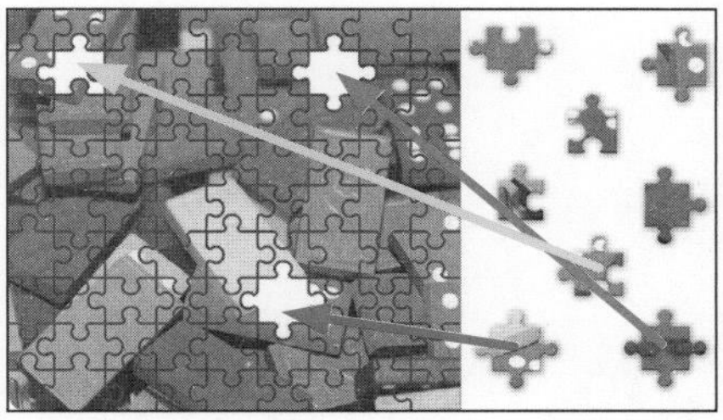

Pages 10–11
Seeing Double

2+3=5 **W**
7+8=15 **U**
10+9=19 **D**
3+4=7 **H**
6+5=11 **O**
5+4=9 **Y**

What do you say when you meet a two-headed space alien?
"HOW DO YOU DO? HOW DO YOU DO?"

7+7=14 6=3+3 10+10=20 8=4+4 6+6=12 18=9+9

Page 12
Reptile Riddle

What do two snakes do after they fight?
THEY HISS AND MAKE UP.

Page 13
Key Problems

What did the pirate get on the test?
A HIGH C

Pages 14–15
Happy Birthday!

6+6=12
3+3=6
10+8=18
5+2=7
3+1=4

1 & 13
4 & 10
2 & 12
5 & 9
7 & 7
3 & 11
6 & 8

Page 16
Flip Flops

3+6=9
7+2=9
8=8+0
1+11=12
18=15+3
2+7=9
18=3+15
6+3=9
11+1=12
8=0+8

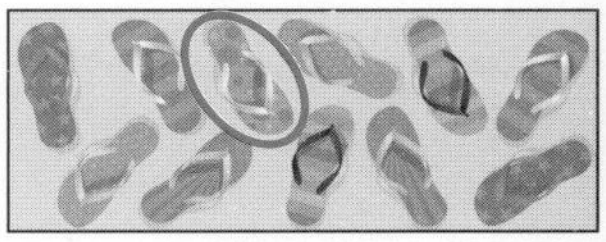

Answers

Page 17
Let's Balance!

$7+7=6+8$ $2+1=3+0$
$9+8=5+12$ $11+1=5+7$
$3+7=5+5$ $11+7=10+8$

Pages 18–19
Take Three

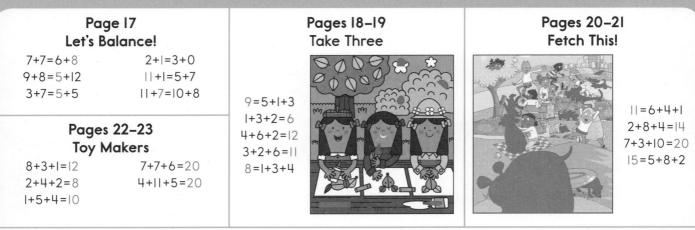

$9=5+1+3$
$1+3+2=6$
$4+6+2=12$
$3+2+6=11$
$8=1+3+4$

Pages 20–21
Fetch This!

$11=6+4+1$
$2+8+4=14$
$7+3+10=20$
$15=5+8+2$

Pages 22–23
Toy Makers

$8+3+1=12$ $7+7+6=20$
$2+4+2=8$ $4+11+5=20$
$1+5+4=10$

Pages 24–25
All in the Family

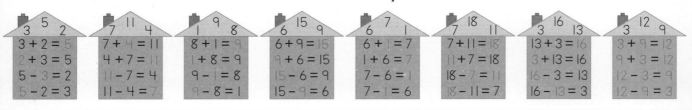

$3+2=5$ $7+4=11$ $8+1=9$ $6+9=15$ $6+1=7$ $7+11=18$ $13+3=16$ $3+9=12$
$2+3=5$ $4+7=11$ $1+8=9$ $9+6=15$ $1+6=7$ $11+7=18$ $3+13=16$ $9+3=12$
$5-3=2$ $11-7=4$ $9-1=8$ $15-6=9$ $7-6=1$ $18-7=11$ $16-3=13$ $12-3=9$
$5-2=3$ $11-4=7$ $9-8=1$ $15-9=6$ $7-1=6$ $18-11=7$ $16-13=3$ $12-9=3$

Pages 26–27
Missing!

$5+1=6$ $8+3=11$
$6-5=1$ $11-8=3$

$7+2=9$ $7+9=16$
$9-7=2$ $16-7=9$

$10+4=14$ $9+9=18$
$14-10=4$ $18-9=9$

$5+12=17$ $9+11=20$
$17-5=12$ $20-9=11$

Pages 28–29
At the Cat Café

$9+3=12$
$4+13=17$
$8+2=10$

Pages 30–31
Guess What?

$6+3=9$ $10+5=15$
$6+8=14$ $12+7=19$
$6+4=10$

candy-corn	320
bow-tie pasta	136
marbles	100
mints	53
toy cars	9